Young People's Workbook
for
Junior Genealogy
Classes

Bee Bartron Koons

Edited by

Carol Davidson Baird
Dorothy Miller
Margaret Fairfield Read

HERITAGE BOOKS
2012

HERITAGE BOOKS

AN IMPRINT OF HERITAGE BOOKS, INC.

Books, CDs, and more—Worldwide

For our listing of thousands of titles see our website
at
www.HeritageBooks.com

Published 2012 by
HERITAGE BOOKS, INC.
Publishing Division
100 Railroad Ave. #104
Westminster, Maryland 21157

Edited in 2004 by the
North San Diego County Genealogical Society
P.O. Box 581
Carlsbad, California 92018-0581

www.cagenweb.com/nsdcgs

Affiliated with
The Georgina Cole Library
1250 Carlsbad Village Drive
Carlsbad, California 92008
Genealogy Desk (760) 434-2931

Other Heritage Books by The Author:
Teaching Genealogy to Young People

International Standard Book Numbers
Paperbound: 978-0-7884-3354-2
Clothbound: 978-0-7884-3439-6

Bee Koons* is a California native, born and raised in San Luis Obispo, CA. Among her many jobs, she was a unit manager for a department of surgery in Arizona. After retiring, she became a teacher of genealogy to both adults and children. Her junior genealogy classes for the North San Diego County Genealogical Society have been an inspiration to other societies all over the country. The uniqueness of her youth class includes her creative concept about the *love line* as well as the blood line of genealogical descent, giving children of adopted or broken families a feeling of inclusion and comfort. She has been a cherished member and volunteer of the NSDCGS for many years and has served on the board of directors in many capacities. Her fifty years of marriage to Earl Koons has produced three children, nine grandchildren, and four great-grandsons. Bee and Earl reside in Fallbrook, CA.

*AKA the "Queen Mother" to Carol Davidson Baird, "Queen" of NSDCGS because of Carol's longest reign as President. Nominated for the position by Bee, it became evident that neither Carol nor anyone else could say no to her. Bee always thought about everyone else and the society before herself, making it a pleasure to say yes to her. I will always love her. CDB

ACKNOWLEDGMENTS

There are many people I wish to thank for their assistance, encouragement and very real and practical endeavors to make the Junior Classes become a reality and this student's manual become a completed accomplishment.

My deep gratitude extends to John Quartarone, Head of the Children's Division at the Carlsbad City Library—Dove Branch, who supplied me with the first forms that we used in the classes, the first class meeting areas and the enthusiasm he showed for these classes to take place. It was due to him and Mary Van Orsdol that we were able to achieve the initial class structures.

Mary Van Orsdol, Head of the Genealogy Division of the Carlsbad City Library, has been supportive and instrumental in making these classes the success that they have been. She has taught the library orientation portion of the Junior Classes from the very first one and is still doing so in the current class structure. Her expertise in the creation of actual exercises for the intermediate classes has been beyond good and has provided the students with the opportunity to actually do a research project using library materials. There are not adequate words to describe my gratitude and appreciation for all that Mary has done and is doing for this ongoing project.

Thanks also go to Suzanne Smithson, Head of the Children's Division at the Carlsbad City Library—Cole Branch, who has provided the access for students to enroll in the Junior Classes and who has enthusiastically supported the project.

Kudos to Margaret Read and Susan Koski for their assistance and support of the Junior Classes, particularly in the past year. The instructor and author is deeply grateful for their support and active participation.

Deep thanks go to the committee that has worked so diligently to complete the necessary editing, formatting, and indexing to prepare the manual and workbook for publication. The committee consisted of Margaret Read, our chairperson and diligent editor, Phyllis Young, our idea person, Carol Davidson Baird, who formatted the manuscript and procured the publisher, and most especially, Dorothy Miller, who indexed the manuscript, created the pedigree, family group sheet and census forms, and assisted with computer technology expertise. They have all done a wonderful job and I am deeply grateful to them all.

Of course, I thank publisher Craig Scott, of Willow Bend Books/Heritage Books, Inc. for agreeing to publish this manual and workbook immediately after being presented with the idea.

And last, but certainly not least, thanks go to all the members of the North San Diego County Genealogical Society who have given me their unending support and encouragement with this project.

Bee Koons

TABLE OF CONTENTS

FAMILY HISTORY

My History

Father's History

Paternal History - Grandfather

Paternal History - Grandmother

Paternal History - Great-Grandfather

Paternal History - Great-Grandmother

Mother's History

Maternal History - Grandfather

Maternal History - Grandmother

Maternal History - Great-Grandfather

Maternal History - Great-Grandmother

MY HISTORY

Full Name_____

Date of Birth_____

Place of Birth _____

City_____County_____State_____Country_____

Size at Birth _____Pounds_____Ounces_____Length

Hair Color_____Eye Color_____

Place of Residence at time of Birth_____

Social Security Number _____

Father's Full Name_____

Father's Birth Date and Place_____

_____

Mother's Full Maiden Name_____

Mother's Birth Date and Place _____

Sibling_____Birth date_____Gender____
Sibling_____Birth date_____Gender____
Sibling_____Birth date_____Gender____

Schools with Dates Attended

_____

_____

Places of Residence with Dates

_____

_____

_____

Honors and
Achievements

_____

Favorite Sports/Hobbies

_____

Organizations Joined

_____

Pets Owned

_____

Best Friends (With my age when I met them)

_____

Important Events in My Life

_____

Special Places I've Visited

_____

FATHER'S HISTORY

Full Name _____ Nickname _____

Date of Birth _____

Place of Birth: City_____ County _____

State_____ Country _____

Size at Birth: _____ Pounds_____ Ounces _____ Length

Hair Color _____ Eye Color_____

Mother's Full Name_____

Father's Full Name_____

Sibling _____ Birthdate _____ Gender____

Sibling _____ Birthdate _____ Gender____

Sibling _____ Birthdate _____ Gender____

Marriage Date and Place_____

City _____County _____State _____

Best Man _____ Usher _____

Usher _____ Usher _____

Person Who Conducted Wedding Ceremony

_____

Schools with Dates Attended

_____

_____

_____

Diplomas and Degrees Achieved

_____

_____

Occupations/Careers/Employment

_____

_____

_____

Military Service

_____

_____

Residences, with Dates

_____

_____

_____

Religious Affiliations

_____

Honors and Achievements

_____

_____

Organizations Joined

_____

_____

_____

_____

Favorite Sports

_____

_____

Favorite Hobbies

_____

_____

_____

Best Friends (Age when they met)

_____

_____

_____

Pets Owned

_____

Vehicles Owned

_____

Important Events in His Life

_____

_____

_____

_____

PATERNAL HISTORY - GRANDFATHER

Full Name _____ Nickname _____

Date of Birth _____

Place of Birth: City_____ County _____

State_____ Country _____

Size at Birth: _____ Pounds _____ Ounces _____ Length

Hair Color _____ Eye Color _____

Mother's Full Name _____

Father's Full Name _____

Sibling _____ Birthdate _____ Gender____

Sibling _____ Birthdate _____ Gender____

Sibling _____ Birthdate _____ Gender____

Marriage Date and Place_____

City _____County _____State_____

Best Man _____ Usher _____

Usher _____ Usher _____

Person Who Conducted Wedding Ceremony
_____

Schools with Dates Attended
_____
_____
_____

Diplomas and Degrees Achieved
_____
_____
_____

Occupations/Careers/Employment
_____
_____
_____

Military Service
_____
_____

Residences, with Dates
_____
_____
_____

DAILY TIMES

Religious Affiliations

_____

_____

Honors and Achievements

_____

_____

_____

Organizations Joined

_____

_____

_____

_____

_____

Favorite Sports

_____

_____

Favorite Hobbies

_____

_____

_____

_____

Best Friends (Age when they met)

_____

_____

_____

_____

Pets Owned

_____

_____

Vehicles Owned

_____

_____

Important Events in His Life

_____

_____

_____

_____

PATERNAL HISTORY - GRANDMOTHER

Full Maiden Name _____ Nickname _____

Date of Birth _____

Place of Birth: City _____ County _____

State _____ Country _____

Size at Birth: _____ Pounds _____ Ounces _____ Length

Hair Color _____ EyeColor _____

Mother's Name _____

Father's Name _____

Sibling _____ Birthdate _____ Gender _____

Sibling _____ Birthdate _____ Gender _____

Sibling _____ Birthdate _____ Gender _____

Marriage Date and Place _____

City _____ County _____ State _____

Maid of Honor _____ Bridesmaid _____

Bridesmaid _____ Bridesmaid _____

Person Who Conducted Wedding Ceremony _____

Schools with Dates Attended

_____

_____

_____

_____

Diplomas and Degrees Achieved

_____

_____

_____

_____

Occupations/Careers/Employment

_____

_____

Residences with Dates

_____

_____

_____

_____

_____

Religious Affiliations

_____

Honors and Achievements

_____

_____

Organizations Joined

_____

_____

_____

Favorite Sports/Hobbies

_____

_____

_____

Collections

_____

_____

Best Friends (Age when they met)

_____

_____

_____

Pets Owned

_____

_____

Important Events in Her Life

_____

_____

_____

_____

_____

PATERNAL HISTORY - GREAT-GRANDFATHER

Full Name _____ Nickname _____

Date of Birth _____

Place of Birth: City _____ County _____

State _____ Country _____

Size at Birth: _____ Pounds _____ Ounces _____ Length

Hair Color _____ Eye Color _____

Mother's Full Name _____

Father's Full Name _____

Sibling _____ Birthdate _____ Gender ____

Sibling _____ Birthdate _____ Gender ____

Sibling _____ Birthdate _____ Gender ____

Marriage Date and Place _____

City _____ County _____ State _____

Best Man _____ Usher _____

Usher _____ Usher _____

Person Who Conducted Wedding Ceremony

_____

Schools with Dates Attended

_____

_____

_____

Diplomas and Degrees Achieved

_____

_____

Occupations/Careers/Employment

_____

_____

_____

Military Service

_____

_____

Residences, with Dates

_____

_____

_____

Religious Affiliations

_____

_____

Honors and Achievements

_____

_____

_____

Organizations Joined

_____

_____

_____

_____

_____

Favorite Sports

_____

_____

Favorite Hobbies

_____

_____

_____

_____

Best Friends (Age when they met)

_____

_____

_____

_____

Pets Owned

_____

Vehicles Owned

_____

_____

Important Events in His Life

_____

_____

_____

_____

PATERNAL HISTORY - GREAT-GRANDMOTHER

Full Maiden Name _____ Nickname _____

Date of Birth _____

Place of Birth: City _____ County _____

State _____ Country _____

Size at Birth: _____ Pounds _____ Ounces _____ Length

Hair Color _____ Eye Color _____

Mother's Name _____

Father's Name _____

Sibling _____ Birthdate _____ Gender ____

Sibling _____ Birthdate _____ Gender ____

Sibling _____ Birthdate _____ Gender ____

Marriage Date and Place _____

City _____ County _____ State _____

Maid of Honor _____ Bridesmaid _____

Bridesmaid _____ Bridesmaid _____

Person Who Conducted Wedding Ceremony

_____

Schools with Dates Attended

_____

_____

_____

_____

Diplomas and Degrees Achieved

_____

_____

_____

_____

Occupations/Careers/Employment

_____

_____

Residences with Dates

_____

_____

_____

_____

_____

Religious Affiliations

_____

Honors and Achievements

_____
_____
_____

Organizations Joined

_____
_____
_____

Favorite Sports/Hobbies

_____
_____
_____

Collections

_____
_____

Best Friends (Age when they met)

_____
_____
_____

Pets Owned

_____

Important Events in Her Life

_____
_____
_____
_____
_____

MOTHER'S HISTORY

Full Maiden Name_____Nickname _____

Date of Birth_____

Place of Birth_____County _____

State_____Country _____

Size at Birth: _____Pounds _____Ounces _____Length

Hair Color _____Eye Color_____

Mother's Full Maiden Name_____

Father's Full Name _____

Sibling _____Birthdate _____Gender ____

Sibling _____Birthdate _____Gender ____

Sibling _____Birthdate _____Gender ____

Marriage Date_____

Marriage Place: City _____County _____State _____

Maid of Honor _____Bridesmaid _____

Bridesmaid _____Bridesmaid _____

Person Who Conducted Wedding Ceremony_____

Schools with Dates Attended

_____

_____

_____

Diplomas and Degrees Achieved

_____

_____

_____

Occupations/Careers/Employment

_____

_____

_____

_____

Military Service

_____

_____

Residences with Dates

_____

_____

_____

Religious Affiliations

_____

Honors and Achievements

_____
_____
_____

Organizations Joined

_____
_____

Favorite Sports

_____
_____

Favorite Hobbies

_____
_____

Best Friends (Age when they met)

_____
_____
_____

Pets Owned

_____
_____

Vehicles Owned

_____

Important Events in Her Life

_____
_____
_____
_____

MATERNAL HISTORY - GRANDFATHER

Full Name _____ Nickname _____

Date of Birth_____

Place of Birth: City_____ County _____

State_____ Country _____

Size at Birth: _____ Pounds _____ Ounces _____ Length

Hair Color _____ Eye Color_____

Mother's Full Name_____

Father's Full Name_____

Sibling _____ Birthdate _____ Gender _____

Sibling _____ Birthdate _____ Gender_____

Sibling _____ Birthdate _____ Gender_____

Marriage Date and Place_____

City _____County _____State_____

Best Man _____ Usher_____

Usher _____ Usher_____

Person Who Conducted Wedding Ceremony_____

Schools with Dates Attended

_____

_____

_____

Diplomas and Degrees Achieved

_____

_____

Occupations/Careers/Employment

_____

_____

_____

Military Service

_____

_____

Residences, with Dates

_____

_____

_____

Religious Affiliations

_____

Honors and Achievements

_____

_____

Organizations Joined

_____

_____

_____

Favorite Sports

_____

_____

Favorite Hobbies

_____

_____

Best Friends (Age when they met)

_____

_____

_____

Pets Owned

_____

Vehicles Owned

_____

Important Events in His Life

_____

_____

_____

MATERNAL HISTORY - GRANDMOTHER

Full Maiden Name _____ Nickname _____

Date of Birth_____

Place of Birth: City _____ County _____

State_____ Country_____

Size at Birth: _____ Pounds _____ Ounces _____ Length

Hair Color _____ Eye Color _____

Mother's Name _____

Father's Name_____

Sibling _____ Birthdate _____ Gender____

Sibling _____ Birthdate _____ Gender____

Sibling _____ Birthdate _____ Gender____

Marriage Date And Place _____

City _____ County _____State_____

Maid of Honor_____ Bridesmaid _____

Bridesmaid _____ Bridesmaid _____

Person Who Conducted Wedding Ceremony_____

Schools with Dates Attended

_____

_____

_____

_____

Diplomas and Degrees Achieved

_____

_____

_____

_____

Occupations/Careers/Employment

_____

_____

Residences with Dates

_____

_____

_____

_____

_____

Religious Affiliations

_____
_____
_____

Honors and Achievements

_____
_____
_____
_____

Organizations Joined

_____
_____
_____
_____

Favorite Sports/Hobbies

_____
_____
_____
_____

Collections

_____
_____
_____

Best Friends (Age when they met)

_____
_____
_____
_____

Pets Owned

_____
_____
_____

Important Events in Her Life

_____
_____
_____
_____
_____

MATERNAL HISTORY - GREAT - GRANDFATHER

Full Name _____ Nickname _____

Date of Birth _____

Place of Birth: City _____ County _____

        State _____ Country _____

Size at Birth: _____ Pounds _____ Ounces _____ Length

Hair Color _____ Eye Color _____

Mother's Full Name _____

Father's Full Name _____

Sibling _____ Birthdate _____ Gender _____

Sibling _____ Birthdate _____ Gender _____

Sibling _____ Birthdate _____ Gender _____

Marriage Date and Place _____

City _____ County _____ State _____

Best Man _____ Usher _____

Usher _____ Usher _____

Person Who Conducted Wedding Ceremony

_____

Schools with Dates Attended

_____

_____

Diplomas and Degrees Achieved

_____

_____

Occupations/Careers/Employment

_____

_____

_____

Military Service

_____

_____

Residences, with Dates

_____

_____

_____

Religious Affiliations

_____

_____

Honors and Achievements

_____

_____

_____

Organizations Joined

_____

_____

_____

_____

Favorite Sports

_____

_____

Favorite Hobbies

_____

_____

_____

Best Friends (Age when they met)

_____

_____

_____

Pets Owned

_____

Vehicles Owned

_____

Important Events in His Life

_____

_____

_____

_____

MATERNAL HISTORY—GREAT-GRANDMOTHER

Full Maiden Name _____ Nickname _____

Date of Birth_____

Place of Birth: City _____ County _____

State_____ Country_____

Size at Birth: _____Pounds_____ Ounces _____ Length

Hair Color _____ Eye Color _____

Mother's Full Name _____

Father's Full Name _____

Sibling _____ Birthdate _____ Gender____

Sibling _____ Birthdate _____ Gender____

Sibling _____ Birthdate _____ Gender____

Marriage Date and Place_____

City _____ County _____ State_____

Maid of Honor_____ Bridesmaid _____

Bridesmaid _____ Bridesmaid _____

Person Who Conducted Wedding Ceremony_____

Schools with Dates Attended

_____

_____

_____

_____

Diplomas and Degrees Achieved

_____

_____

_____

Occupations/Careers/Employment

_____

_____

Residences with Dates

_____

_____

_____

_____

Religious Affiliations

_____

_____

Honors and Achievements

_____

_____

_____

Organizations Joined

_____

_____

_____

Favorite Sports/Hobbies

_____

_____

_____

Collections

_____

_____

Best Friends (Age when they met)

_____

_____

_____

Pets Owned

_____

_____

Important Events in Her Life

_____

_____

_____

_____

ORAL HISTORIES

SAMPLE QUESTIONS

ORAL HISTORY RECORD

ADDITIONAL PAGE - ORAL HISTORY RECORD

SAMPLE QUESTIONS FOR
ORAL HISTORY INTERVIEWS

1. How did you and your spouse meet?

2. Where were you and your spouse living when you met?

3. Where did you get married? (Church, judge's office, home)

4. Who attended your wedding?

5. Who were your witnesses at your wedding?

6. Where did you live when you were first married?

7. Where were you living when each of your children were born?

8. Where did your parents live when you were born?

9. Where did you go to school?

10. Who were your sisters and brothers?

11. Did you move a lot when you were growing up?

12. Did your parents have brothers and sisters?

13. Where did your parents marry? When did they marry?

14. Did you have aunts and uncles that lived close to you?

15. Did you have pets when you were young? If so, what were they?

16. What kinds of jobs did you have during your lifetime?

17. Who was your first love? Where did you meet?

18. What kinds of games did you play when you were young?

19. Were you ever in the military? What branch? Did you serve during any war?

SAMPLE QUESTIONS
Continued

20. What do you remember about your grandparents?

21. Did you ever do anything that got you in trouble?

22. As a child, how did you celebrate the holidays, including birthdays?

23. Are there any family heirlooms that have been handed down in the family?

24. Did you ever win an award for academics or sports?

25. Have you ever met anyone famous?

26. Did you ever play a musical instrument, or sing in a choir?

27.
_____

_____

28.
_____

_____

29.
_____

_____

30.
_____

_____

ORAL HISTORY RECORD

Date of Interview_____

Person Being Interviewed_____
Birthdate of Person Being Interviewed _____
Birthplace of Person Being Interviewed:
City_____County_____State_____Country_____

Place of Interview _____

Question Asked_____
_____
Answer _____
_____
_____

Question Asked_____
_____
Answer _____
_____
_____

Question Asked_____
_____
Answer _____
_____
_____

Further Notes _____
_____
_____
_____
_____
_____

Was a type of recorder used? Tape recorder?
Camcorder? Digital recorder?

_____

ADDITIONAL PAGE/ORAL HISTORY

Person Being Interviewed _____

Page Number _____ Date _____

Question _____

Answer _____
_____

Question _____

Answer _____
_____

Question _____

Answer _____
_____

Question _____

Answer _____
_____

Question _____

Answer _____
_____

Question _____

Answer _____
_____

Other Notes _____
_____
_____

ONGOING HISTORY

Family Weddings

Family Photographs

Family Births

Family Deaths

Family Vacations

Family Gatherings

Family Traditions

Family Heirlooms

Family Signatures

FAMILY WEDDINGS

Bride_____Groom _____
Maid of Honor_____Best Man _____
Bridesmaid_____Usher_____
Flower Girl_____Ring Bearer _____
Date _____Time _____
Place _____
Person Who Conducted Ceremony _____
Place of Reception _____
Place of Honeymoon _____
Notes_____
_____
_____
_____
_____
_____
_____

Bride_____Groom _____
Maid of Honor_____Best Man _____
Bridesmaid_____Usher_____
Flower Girl_____Ring Bearer _____
Date _____Time _____
Place _____
Person Who Conducted Ceremony _____
Place of Reception _____
Place of Honeymoon _____
Notes_____
_____
_____
_____
_____
_____

PHOTOGRAPHS

FAMILY BIRTHS

Name_____Date_____Time_____
Weight_____Pounds_____Ounces   Length _____
Hair Color_____   Eye Color_____
Mother_____   Father_____
Place of Birth _____
Residence Address _____
Notes_____
_____
_____

Name_____Date_____Time_____
Weight_____Pounds_____Ounces   Length _____
Hair Color_____   Eye Color_____
Mother_____   Father_____
Place of Birth _____
Residence Address _____
Notes_____
_____
_____

Name_____Date_____Time_____
Weight_____Pounds_____Ounces   Length _____
Hair Color_____   Eye Color_____
Mother_____   Father _____
Place of Birth _____
Residence Address _____
Notes_____
_____
_____

FAMILY DEATHS

Name_____

Date of Death _____ Time of Death _____

Place of Death_____

Place of Residence _____

Cause of Death_____

Place of Burial_____

Date of Burial _____

Father's Name_____

Mother's Name (Including maiden name)

_____

Survivors

_____

_____

Notes_____

_____

_____

_____

Name_____

Date of Death _____ Time of Death _____

Place of Death_____

Place of Residence _____

Cause of Death _____

Place of Burial _____

Date of Burial _____

Father's Name_____

Mother's Name (including maiden name)

_____

Survivors

_____

_____

Notes_____

_____

_____

_____

FAMILY VACATIONS

Place of Vacation _____

Date(s) of Vacation _____

Type of Transportation Used _____

People in the Vacation Party _____

_____

_____

_____

Purpose of Vacation _____

Notes _____

_____

_____

_____

Place of Vacation _____

Date(s) of Vacation _____

Type of Transportation Used _____

People in the Vacation Party _____

_____

_____

Purpose of Vacation _____

Notes _____

_____

_____

_____

Place of Vacation _____

Date(s) of Vacation _____

Type of Transportation Used _____

People in the Vacation Party _____

_____

_____

Purpose of Vacation _____

Notes _____

_____

_____

FAMILY GATHERINGS

Occasion for Gathering_____

Date and Time of Event _____

Place of Event_____

People Who Attended

_____

_____

_____

_____

Notes_____

_____

_____

_____

_____

_____

Occasion for Gathering_____

Date and Time of Event _____

Place of Event_____

People Who Attended

_____

_____

_____

_____

Notes_____

_____

_____

_____

_____

_____

FAMILY TRADITIONS

Tradition

_____

_____

When Tradition is Observed

_____

_____

How Many Generations Has Tradition Been Done? _____

Do Descendants Plan on Continuing Tradition?_____

If not, why not?_____

Notes_____

_____

_____

Tradition _____

_____

When Tradition is Observed

_____

_____

How Many Generations Has Tradition Been Done? _____

Do Descendants Plan on Continuing Tradition?_____

If not, why not?_____

Notes_____

_____

_____

Tradition

_____

_____

When Tradition is Observed

_____

_____

How Many Generations Has Tradition Been Done? _____

Do Descendants Plan on Continuing Tradition?_____

If not, why not?_____

Notes_____

_____

_____

FAMILY HEIRLOOMS

Heirloom
_____

Owner of Heirloom_____
Location of Heirloom _____
Original Owner of Heirloom_____
Number of Generations in Family _____
Notes_____

_____
_____
_____

Heirloom
_____

Owner of Heirloom_____
Location of Heirloom _____
Original Owner of Heirloom_____
Number of Generations in Family _____
Notes_____

_____
_____
_____

Heirloom
_____

Owner of Heirloom_____
Location of Heirloom _____
Original Owner of Heirloom_____
Number of Generations in Family _____
Notes_____

_____
_____
_____

FAMILY SIGNATURES

Signature
_____

Printed Name _____
Date of Signature _____
Place of Signature_____
Residence of Signer _____
Relationship to Collector _____

Signature
_____

Printed Name _____
Date of Signature _____
Place of Signature_____
Residence of Signer _____
Relationship to Collector _____

Signature
_____

Printed Name _____
Date of Signature_____
Place of Signature_____
Residence of Signer _____
Relationship to Collector _____

Signature _____

Printed Name _____
Date of Signature _____
Place of Signature_____
Residence of Signer _____
Relationship to Collector _____

IMPORTANT FAMILY EVENTS

January

February

March

April

May

June

July

August

September

October

November

December

IMPORTANT FAMILY EVENTS

JANUARY

1 _____   16 _____

2 _____   17 _____

3 _____   18 _____

4 _____   19 _____

5 _____   20 _____

6 _____   21 _____

7 _____   22 _____

8 _____   23 _____

9 _____   24 _____

10 _____   25 _____

11 _____   26 _____

12 _____   27 _____

13 _____   28 _____

14 _____   29 _____

15 _____   30 _____

                                 31 _____

_____

_____

_____

_____

_____

IMPORTANT FAMILY EVENTS

FEBRUARY

1_____

2_____

3_____

4_____

5_____

6_____

7_____

8_____

9_____

10_____

11_____

12_____

13_____

14_____

15_____

16_____

17_____

18_____

19_____

20_____

21_____

22_____

23_____

24_____

25_____

26_____

27_____

28_____

29_____

_____

_____

_____

_____

_____

IMPORTANT FAMILY EVENTS

MARCH

1 _____	16 _____
2 _____	17 _____
3 _____	18 _____
4 _____	19 _____
5 _____	20 _____
6 _____	21 _____
7 _____	22 _____
8 _____	23 _____
9 _____	24 _____
10 _____	25 _____
11 _____	26 _____
12 _____	27 _____
13 _____	28 _____
14 _____	29 _____
15 _____	30 _____
	31 _____

_____
_____
_____
_____
_____

IMPORTANT FAMILY EVENTS

APRIL

1 _____   16 _____
2 _____   17 _____
3 _____   18 _____
4 _____   19 _____
5 _____   20 _____
6 _____   21 _____
7 _____   22 _____
8 _____   23 _____
9 _____   24 _____
10 _____   25 _____
11 _____   26 _____
12 _____   27 _____
13 _____   28 _____
14 _____   29 _____
15 _____   30 _____

_____
_____
_____
_____
_____

IMPORTANT FAMILY EVENTS

MAY

1 _____

2 _____

3 _____

4 _____

5 _____

6 _____

7 _____

8 _____

9 _____

10 _____

11 _____

12 _____

13 _____

14 _____

15 _____

16 _____

17 _____

18 _____

19 _____

20 _____

21 _____

22 _____

23 _____

24 _____

25 _____

26 _____

27 _____

28 _____

29 _____

30 _____

31 _____

_____

_____

_____

_____

_____

IMPORTANT FAMILY EVENTS

JUNE

1_____		16_____	
2_____		17_____	
3_____		18_____	
4_____		19_____	
5_____		20_____	
6_____		21_____	
7_____		22_____	
8_____		23_____	
9_____		24_____	
10_____		25_____	
11_____		26_____	
12_____		27_____	
13_____		28_____	
14_____		29_____	
15_____		30_____	

_____
_____
_____
_____
_____

IMPORTANT FAMILY EVENTS

JULY

1 _____

2 _____

3 _____

4 _____

5 _____

6 _____

7 _____

8 _____

9 _____

10 _____

11 _____

12 _____

13 _____

14 _____

15 _____

16 _____

17 _____

18 _____

19 _____

20 _____

21 _____

22 _____

23 _____

24 _____

25 _____

26 _____

27 _____

28 _____

29 _____

30 _____

31 _____

_____

_____

_____

_____

_____

IMPORTANT FAMILY EVENTS

AUGUST

1 _____
2 _____
3 _____
4 _____
5 _____
6 _____
7 _____
8 _____
9 _____
10 _____
11 _____
12 _____
13 _____
14 _____
15 _____

16 _____
17 _____
18 _____
19 _____
20 _____
21 _____
22 _____
23 _____
24 _____
25 _____
26 _____
27 _____
28 _____
29 _____
30 _____
31 _____

_____
_____
_____
_____
_____

IMPORTANT FAMILY EVENTS

SEPTEMBER

1 _____

2 _____

3 _____

4 _____

5 _____

6 _____

7 _____

8 _____

9 _____

10 _____

11 _____

12 _____

13 _____

14 _____

15 _____

16 _____

17 _____

18 _____

19 _____

20 _____

21 _____

22 _____

23 _____

24 _____

25 _____

26 _____

27 _____

28 _____

29 _____

30 _____

_____

_____

_____

_____

_____

IMPORTANT FAMILY EVENTS

OCTOBER

1_____

2_____

3_____

4_____

5_____

6_____

7_____

8_____

9_____

10_____

11_____

12_____

13_____

14_____

15_____

16_____

17_____

18_____

19_____

20_____

21_____

22_____

23_____

24_____

25_____

26_____

27_____

28_____

29_____

30_____

31_____

_____

_____

_____

_____

_____

IMPORTANT FAMILY EVENTS

NOVEMBER

1_____   16_____

2_____   17_____

3_____   18_____

4_____   19_____

5_____   20_____

6_____   21_____

7_____   22_____

8_____   23_____

9_____   24_____

10_____   25_____

11_____   26_____

12_____   27_____

13_____   28_____

14_____   29_____

15_____   30_____

_____

_____

_____

_____

_____

_____

IMPORTANT FAMILY EVENTS

DECEMBER

1 _____
2 _____
3 _____
4 _____
5 _____
6 _____
7 _____
8 _____
9 _____
10 _____
11 _____
12 _____
13 _____
14 _____
15 _____

16 _____
17 _____
18 _____
19 _____
20 _____
21 _____
22 _____
23 _____
24 _____
25 _____
26 _____
27 _____
28 _____
29 _____
30 _____
31 _____

_____
_____
_____
_____
_____
_____

PHOTOGRAPHS

PHOTOGRAPHS

PEDIGREE CHARTS

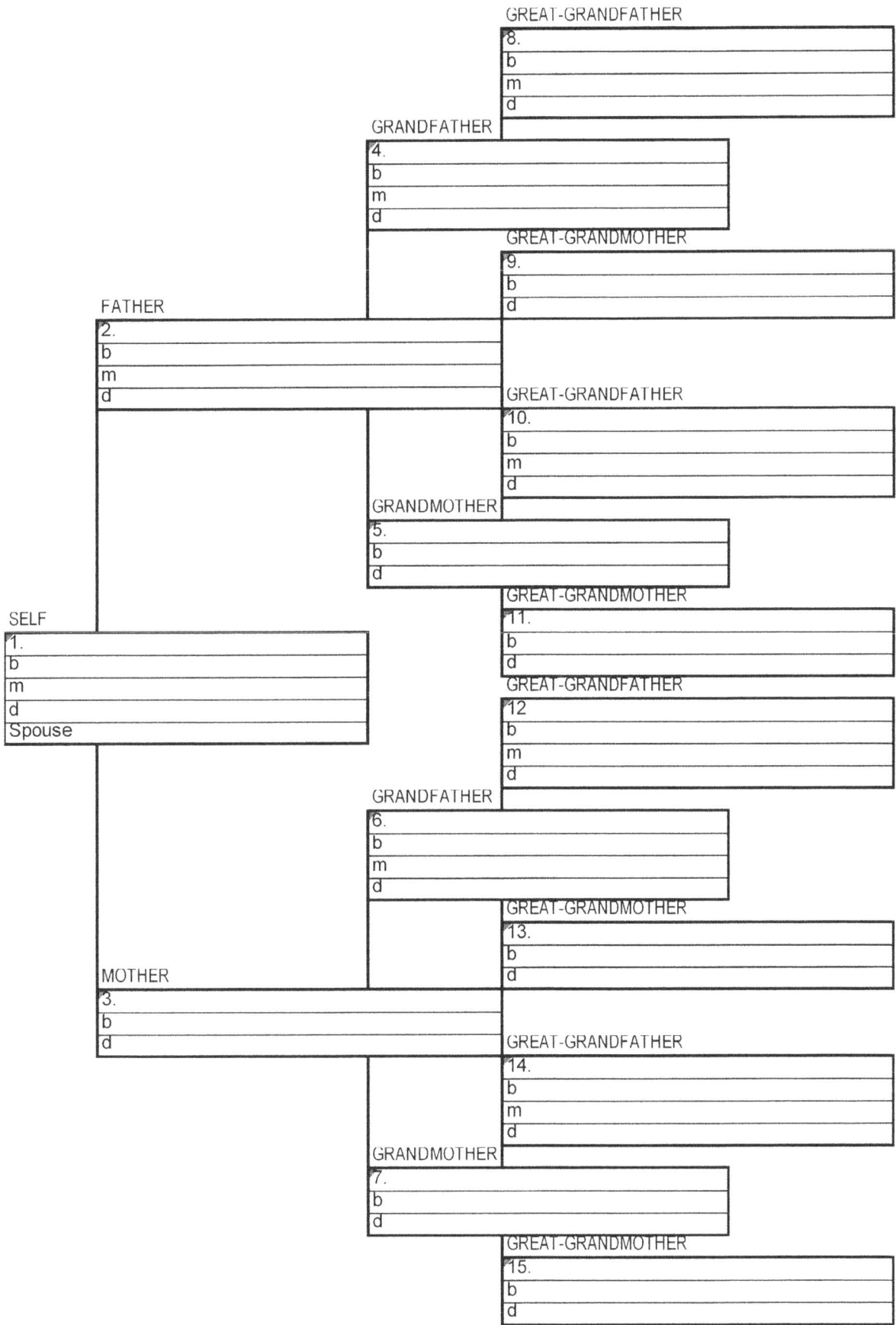

GREAT-GRANDFATHER

8.	
b	
m	
d	

GRANDFATHER

4.	
b	
m	
d	

GREAT-GRANDMOTHER

9.	
b	
d	

FATHER

2.	
b	
m	
d	

GREAT-GRANDFATHER

10.	
b	
m	
d	

GRANDMOTHER

5.	
b	
d	

GREAT-GRANDMOTHER

11.	
b	
d	

SELF

1.	
b	
m	
d	
Spouse	

GREAT-GRANDFATHER

12	
b	
m	
d	

GRANDFATHER

6.	
b	
m	
d	

GREAT-GRANDMOTHER

13.	
b	
d	

MOTHER

3.	
b	
d	

GREAT-GRANDFATHER

14.	
b	
m	
d	

GRANDMOTHER

7.	
b	
d	

GREAT-GRANDMOTHER

15.	
b	
d	

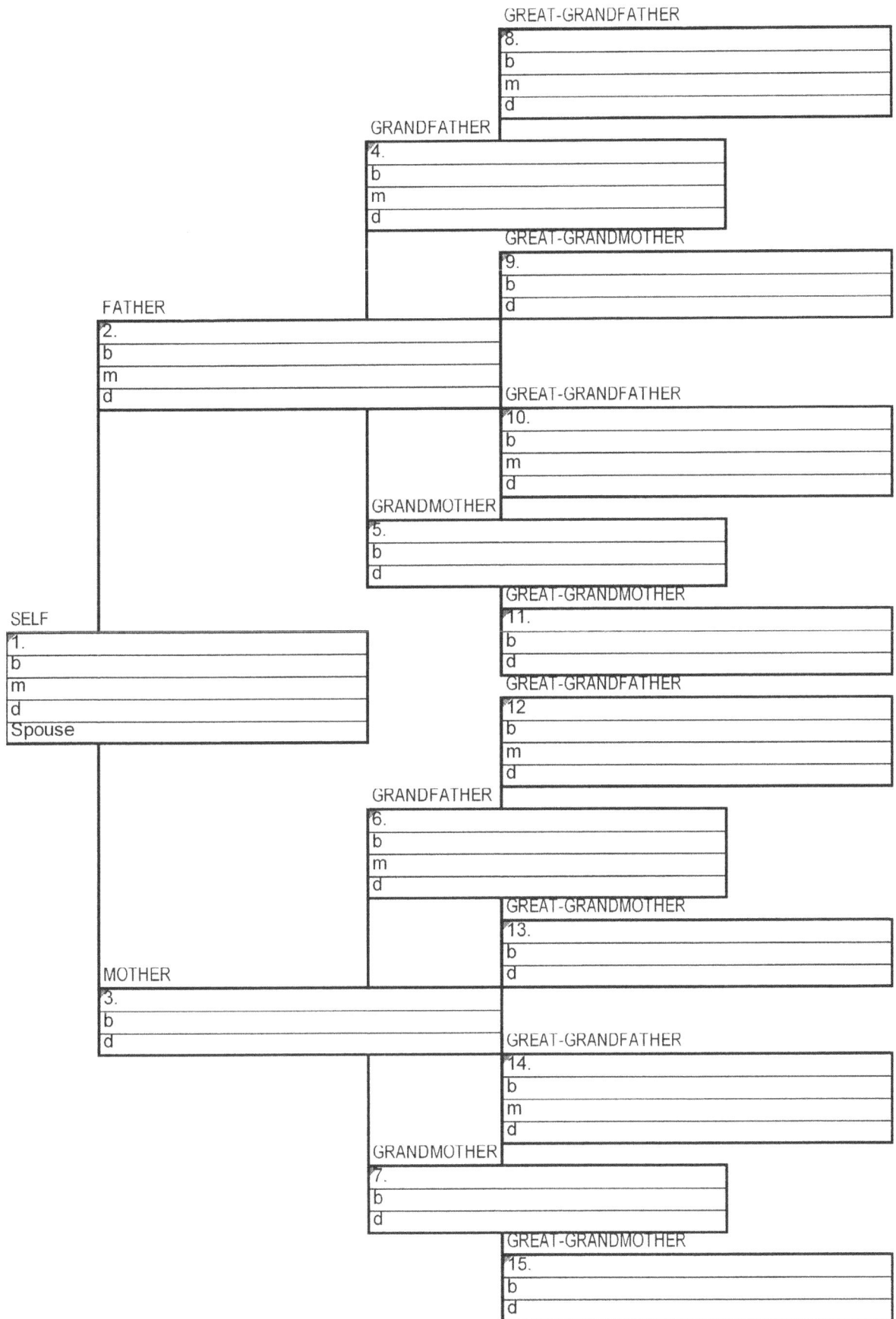

GREAT-GRANDFATHER

8.
b
m
d

GRANDFATHER

4.
b
m
d

GREAT-GRANDMOTHER

9.
b
d

FATHER

2.
b
m
d

GREAT-GRANDFATHER

10.
b
m
d

GRANDMOTHER

5.
b
d

GREAT-GRANDMOTHER

11.
b
d

SELF

1.
b
m
d
Spouse

GREAT-GRANDFATHER

12
b
m
d

GRANDFATHER

6.
b
m
d

GREAT-GRANDMOTHER

13.
b
d

MOTHER

3.
b
d

GREAT-GRANDFATHER

14.
b
m
d

GRANDMOTHER

7.
b
d

GREAT-GRANDMOTHER

15.
b
d

FAMILY GROUP SHEETS

Family Group Sheet

Father	FULL NAME	
EVENT	DAY MONTH YEAR	PLACE OF EVENT (City, Township, County, State or Country)
Birth		
Marriage		
Death		
Burial		

NOTES:

His Other Spouse(s)			
His Father:		Born:	Died:
His Mother:		Born:	Died:

Mother	FULL MAIDEN NAME:	
EVENT	DAY MONTH YEAR	PLACE OF EVENT (City, Township, County, State or Country)
Birth		
Death		
Burial		

NOTES:

Her Other Spouse(s)			
Her Father:		Born:	Died:
Her Mother:		Born:	Died:

Children (given name)		DAY MONTH YEAR	PLACE OF EVENT	NAME OF SPOUSE(S)
1	b			
	m			
	d			
2	b			
	m			
	d			
3	b			
	m			
	d			
4	b			
	m			
	d			
5	b			
	m			
	d			
6	b			
	m			
	d			
7	b			
	m			
	d			
8	b			
	m			
	d			
9	b			
	m			
	d			
10	b			
	m			
	d			
11	b			
	m			
	d			
12	b			
	m			
	d			

References

Itemize each source used to document names, dates, and places for each member of the family

Page Source	Type of Record	In Reference To	Information Given

Family Group Sheet

Father	FULL NAME	
EVENT	DAY MONTH YEAR	PLACE OF EVENT (City, Township, County, State or Country)
Birth		
Marriage		
Death		
Burial		

NOTES:

His Other Spouse(s)			
His Father:		Born:	Died:
His Mother:		Born:	Died:

Mother	FULL MAIDEN NAME:	
EVENT	DAY MONTH YEAR	PLACE OF EVENT (City, Township, County, State or Country)
Birth		
Death		
Burial		

NOTES:

Her Other Spouse(s)			
Her Father:		Born:	Died:
Her Mother:		Born:	Died:

Children (given name)		DAY MONTH YEAR	PLACE OF EVENT	NAME OF SPOUSE(S)
1	b			
	m			
	d			
2	b			
	m			
	d			
3	b			
	m			
	d			
4	b			
	m			
	d			
5	b			
	m			
	d			
6	b			
	m			
	d			
7	b			
	m			
	d			
8	b			
	m			
	d			
9	b			
	m			
	d			
10	b			
	m			
	d			
11	b			
	m			
	d			
12	b			
	m			
	d			

References

Itemize each source used to document names, dates, and places for each member of the family

Page Source	Type of Record	In Reference To	Information Given

CENSUS RECORD SHEETS

1790 Federal Census

1800 Federal Census

1810 Federal Census

1820 Federal Census

1830 Federal Census

1840 Federal Census

1850 Federal Census

1860 Federal Census

1870 Federal Census

1880 Federal Census

1890 Veterans Schedule

1900 Federal Census

1910 Federal Census

1920 Federal Census

1930 Federal Census

1790 Federal Census

Researcher: Date:

Heads of household extracted from the original text of the 1790 Population Schedules

NARA Microfilm Series M637 Roll no : Page no: STATE & COUNTY	Name of HEAD OF HOUSEHOLD	FREE WHITES			Slaves	Other free persons
		Males 16 & over	Males 0 - 15	Females		

1800 Federal Census

Researcher: Date:

Heads of household extracted from the original text of the 1800 Population Schedules

NARA Microfilm Series M32   Roll no: State: County: Township:

Page	Name of HEAD OF HOUSEHOLD	FREE WHITE MALES					FREE WHITE FEMALES					Other free persons	Slaves
		0 thru 9	10 thru 15	16 thru 25	26 thru 44	45 and over	0 thru 9	10 thru 15	16 thru 25	26 thru 44	45 and over		

1810 Federal Census

Researcher: Date:

Heads of household extracted from the original text of the 1800 Population Schedules

NARA Microfilm Series M252   Roll no: State: County: Township:

Page	Name of HEAD OF HOUSEHOLD	FREE WHITE MALES					FREE WHITE FEMALES					Other free persons	Slaves
		0 thru 9	10 thru 15	16 thru 25	26 thru 44	45 and over	0 thru 9	10 thru 15	16 thru 25	26 thru 44	45 and over		

1820 Federal Census

Heads of households extracted from the original text of the 1820 Population Schedules

Researcher: _____   Date: _____

NARA Microfilm Series M33   Roll no: _____   State: _____   County: _____   Township: _____

Page	Name of HEAD OF HOUSEHOLD	FREE WHITES												Foreigners not naturalized	No. of persons engaged in			SLAVES								FREE COLORED								All other persons
		Males						Females							Agriculture	Commerce	Manufacture	Males				Females				Males				Females				
		0 thru 9 years	10 thru 15 years	16 thru 18 years	19 thru 25 years	26 thru 44 years	45 years and over	0 thru 9 years	10 thru 15 years	16 thru 18 years	19 thru 25 years	26 thru 44 years	45 years and over					0 thru 13 years	14 thru 25 years	26 thru 44 years	45 years and over	0 thru 13 years	14 thru 25 years	26 thru 44 years	45 years and over	0 thru 13 years	14 thru 25 years	26 thru 44 years	45 years and over	0 thru 13 years	14 thru 25 years	26 thru 44 years	45 years and over	

1830 Federal Census

Extracted from the original text of the 1830 Census Schedules

NARA Microfilm Series M19

Roll no:

Page:

Researcher:

Date:

State:

County:

Township:

Name of HEAD OF HOUSEHOLD

FREE WHITE PERSONS - including heads of families

Males
- 0 thru 4 years
- 5 thru 9 years
- 10 thru 14 years
- 15 thru 19 years
- 20 thru 29 years
- 30 thru 39 years
- 40 thru 49 years
- 50 thru 59 years
- 60 thru 69 years
- 70 thru 79 years
- 80 thru 89 years
- 90 thru 99 years
- 100 years and over

Females
- 0 thru 4 years
- 5 thru 9 years
- 10 thru 14 years
- 15 thru 19 years
- 20 thru 29 years
- 30 thru 39 years
- 40 thru 49 years
- 50 thru 59 years
- 60 thru 69 years
- 70 thru 79 years
- 80 thru 89 years
- 90 thru 99 years
- 100 years and over

FREE COLORED

Males
- 0 thru 9 years
- 10 thru 23 years
- 24 thru 35 years
- 36 thru 54 years
- 55 thru 99 years
- 100 years and over

Females
- 0 thru 9 years
- 10 thru 23 years
- 24 thru 35 years
- 36 thru 54 years
- 55 thru 99 years
- 100 years and over

TOTAL PERSONS

White persons who are

Deaf & Dumb
- 0 - 13
- 14 - 24
- 25 & OVER

Blind

Aliens

Other information

SLAVES

Males

Females

NOTES

1
2
3
4
5
6
7
8

1840 Federal Census

Researcher:

Date:

Extracted from the original text of the 1840 Census Schedules

NARA Microfilm Series M704   Roll no:

Page: State: County: Township:

Name of HEAD OF HOUSEHOLD

FREE WHITE PERSONS – including heads of families

Males: 0 thru 4 years, 5 thru 9 years, 10 thru 14 years, 15 thru 19 years, 20 thru 29 years, 30 thru 39 years, 40 thru 49 years, 50 thru 59 years, 60 thru 69 years, 70 thru 79 years, 80 thru 89 years, 90 thru 99 years, 100 years and over

Females: 0 thru 4 years, 5 thru 9 years, 10 thru 14 years, 15 thru 19 years, 20 thru 29 years, 30 thru 39 years, 40 thru 49 years, 50 thru 59 years, 60 thru 69 years, 70 thru 79 years, 80 thru 89 years, 90 thru 99 years, 100 years and over

FREE COLORED

Males: 0 thru 9 years, 10 thru 23 years, 24 thru 35 years, 36 thru 54 years, 55 thru 99 years, 100 years and over

Females: 0 thru 9 years, 10 thru 23 years, 24 thru 35 years, 36 thru 54 years, 55 thru 99 years, 100 years and over

TOTAL PERSONS

White persons who are Deaf & Dumb: 0 - 13, 14 - 24, 25 & OVER; Blind; Aliens

Rows: 1, 2, 3, 4, 5, 6, 7, 8

SLAVES

Males

Females

Rows: 1, 2, 3, 4, 5, 6, 7, 8

Schools etc.

Revolutionary War/ Military Pensioners

Name   Age

No. of Persons in Each Family Employed in:

Mining | Agriculture | Commerce | Manufactures and trades | Navigation of the ocean | Navigation of canals, lakes and rivers | Learned professions and engineers

Rows: 1, 2, 3, 4, 5, 6, 7, 8

1850 Federal Census

Extracted from the original text of the 1850 Census Schedules

Researcher:

Date:

NARA Microfilm Series M432   Roll no: State: County: Township:

Page:

| 1 | 2 | 3 | Description | | | 7 | 8 | 9 | 10 | 11 | 12 | 13 |
Dwelling-house no.	Family no.	Name of Person	Age	Sex	Color	Occupation	Value of real estate	Birthplace	Married within year	Attended school	Cannot read or write	Whether deaf and dumb, blind, insane, idiotic, pauper, or convict
1	2	3	4	5	6	7	8	9	10	11	12	13

1860 Federal Census

NARA Microfilm Series M653   Roll no:

Researcher:

Date:

Extracted from the original text of the 1860 Census Schedules

Page: State: County: Township:

Dwelling-house no.	Family no.	Name of Person	Description			Occupation	Value of Estate		Birthplace	Married within year	Attended school	Cannot read or write	Whether deaf and dumb, blind, insane, idiotic, pauper, or convict
			Age	Sex	Color		Real estate	Personal estate					
1	2	3	4	5	6	7	8	9	10	11	12	13	14

1870 Federal Census

NARA Microfilm Series M593   Roll no:

Researcher: Date:

Extracted from the original text of the 1870 Census Schedules

Page: State: County: Township:

Dwelling-house no. 1	Family no. 2	Name of Person 3	Age 4	Sex 5	Color 6	Occupation 7	Value of real estate 8	Personal estate 9	Birthplace 10	Father of foreign birth 11	Mother of foreign birth 12	If born within year 13	If married within year 14	Attended school 15	Cannot read 16	Cannot write 17	Whether deaf and dumb, blind, insane, or idiots 18	Male over 21 19	Denied vote 20

1880 Federal Census

NARA Microfilm Series T9   Roll no: Researcher: Date:

E.D. ____   Page ____   State: ____   County: ____   Township: ____

Street	House no.	Dwelling no.	Family no.	Name of Person	Personal			If born within year	Relationship to Head	Civil Condition			If married within year	Occupation		Health						Education			Birthplace		
					Color	Sex	Age			Single	Married	Widowed/Divorced		Profession or Trade	Months Unemployed	Sickness/Disability	Blind	Deaf or dumb	Idiotic	Insane	Crippled, Etc.	Attended school	Cannot read	Cannot write	Person	Father	Mother
	1	2	3		4	5	6	7	8	9	10	11	12	13	14	15	16	17	18	19	20	21	22	23	24	25	26

In cities

1890 Veterans Schedule

Extracted from the original text of the 1890 special schedules for surviving soldiers, sailors, marines, and widows

Researcher:

Date:

NARA Microfilm Series M123   Roll no: State: County:

House no.	Family no.	Name of surviving soldiers, sailors, marines, or widows	Rank	Company	Name of Regiment or Vessel	Date of enlistment			Date of discharge			Length of service		
1	2	3	4	5	6	day	month	year	day	month	year	day	month	year
						7			8			9		
1														
2														
3														
4														
5														
6														
7														
8														
9														
10														

	Post Office address	Disability incurred	Remarks
1			
2			
3			
4			
5			
6			
7			
8			
9			
10			

1900 Federal Census

Researcher: Date:

Extracted from the original text of the 1900 Census Schedules

NARA Microfilm Series T623   Roll no:

City/Tow n: State: County: Subdistrict:

Page ___ E.D. ___   Ward:

Street	House no. 1	Family no. 2	Name of every person whose place of abode on 1 June 1900 was in this family 3	Relationship to Head 4	Color or race 5	Sex 6	Date of birth Month 7	Date of birth Year 8	Age last birthday 9	Marital status 10	Years married 11	Children born 12	Children living 13	Birthplace of Person 14	Birthplace of Father 15	Birthplace of Mother 16	Year of immigration 17	Number of years in U.S. 18	Naturalization 19	Occupation 20	Months not employed 21	Months at school 22	Can read 23	Can write 24	Can speak English 25	Own/Rent 26	Free/Mortgaged 27	Farm/House 28	No. of farm schedule 29

1910 Federal Census

Date:

Researcher:

Extracted from the original text of the 1910 Census Schedules

NARA Microfilm Series T624   Roll no:

City/Town   Ward:

Page   E.D

State: County: Subdistrict:

Street	House no.	Family no.	Name of Person	Relationship to Head	Sex	Color or Race	Age last birthday	Marital Status	Years married	Children born	Children living	Birthplace of Person	Father	Mother	Year of immigration	Naturalization	Language Spoken	Trade or Profession	Type of business/ Employer, employee, or works on own account	Out of work/Weeks out	Can read	Can write	Attended school	Owned/Rented	Free/Mortgaged	Farm/House	Farm Schedule no.	Veteran	Blind	Deaf
	1	2	3	4	5	6	7	8	9	10	11	12	13	14	15	16	17	18	19 20	21	23	24	25	26	27	28	29	30	31	32

Personal Description

Occupation

Education

Home Ownership

1920 Federal Census

Researcher:

Date:

Extracted from the original text of the 1920 Census Schedules

NARA Microfilm Series T625   Roll no:

State: County: Subdistrict:

City/Town   Ward:

Page   E.D

1	2	3	4	5	6	7	8	9	10	11	12	13	14	15	16	17	18	19	20	21	22	23	24	25	26	27	28	29
Street address	House no.	Dwelling no.	Family no.	Name of Person	Relationship to Head	Owned/Rented	Free/Mortgaged	Sex	Color or Race	Age last birthday	Marital Status	Year of immigration	Naturalization	Year naturalized	Can read	Can write	Attended school	Place of birth	Mother tongue	Place of birth	Mother tongue	Place of birth	Mother tongue	Speaks English?	Trade or Profession	Type of business	works on own account	No. of farm schedule
																		Person		Father		Mother				Employer, employee, or		
												Citizenship			Education			Nativity and mother tongue							Occupation			
						Personal																						

1930 Federal Census

Extracted from the original text of the 1930 Census Schedules

NARA Microfilm Series

Researcher:

Date:

Roll No.

State:

Incorporated place:

Enumeration district no.:

Street no.

County:

Ward of city:

Block no.:

Supervisor's district no.:

Township, Town, Precinct, etc.:

Place of Abode				Name	Relationship to Head	Home data				Personal description					Education		person enumerated and of his or her parents.							Occupation and Industry								
Street, Ave., road, etc.	House no. (in cities)	No. of house order of enumeration	Family no.	Each person whose place of abode on April 1, 1930 was in this family.	Relationship to Head	House owned or rented	Value of home/ monthly payment	Radio set	Live on Farm?	Sex	Color or Race	Age last birthday	Marital Condition	Age, 1st marriage	Attended school	Can read & write	Person	Father	Mother	Language spoken in home before coming to U.S.	Year of immigration to U.S.	Naturalization	Speaks English	Trade or profession or kind of work	Industry or business	Census office code	Class of work	At work yesterday?	Unemployment Schedule No.	Veteran?	What war?	No. Farm schedule
1	2	3	4	5	6	7	8	9	10	11	12	13	14	15	16	17	18	19	20	21	22	23	24	25	26	D	27	28	29	30	31	32

INDEX

www.ingramcontent.com/pod-product-compliance
Lightning Source LLC
Chambersburg PA
CBHW081157270326
41930CB00014B/3190